He Found Me

Based on a true story about a big-hearted island dog from Panama

Written by Kate Bitters, told by Dobby

Myrddin Publishing
United Kingdom | Australia | United States

Copyright © 2017 by Kate Leibfried, writing as Kate Bitters

All rights reserved. This book or any portion thereof may not be reproduced or used in any manner whatsoever without the express written permission of the publisher except for the use of brief quotations in a book review.

Printed in the United States of America

First Printing, 2017

ISBN 13: 978-1-68063-062-6

Myrddin Publishing
Jackson, NJ
United Kingdom | Australia | United States

www.MyrddinPublishing.com

Author's website: www.KateBitters.com

To Dobby

Thank you for choosing me.

My Home

I was born without a name.

Names are only given to dogs who have humans. My mother didn't have a human, and neither did her pups.

We lived together on a tropical island off the coast of Panama. The island was small and surrounded by the turquoise waters of the ocean. My mother lived in the jungle on the outskirts of the only town. She only dared to enter town when she was hungry and needed to steal food from trash cans or relax in the cool dirt by the houses. When she had her litter of black-and-tan-colored puppies, she kept us far away from town in a hidden patch of bushes. My mother feared humans and wanted to protect her puppies as best she could.

"They are unpredictable," Mother said, "especially the little humans. You never know what they will do."

My brothers and sisters and I learned to be cautious around people. We would sneak into town, grab a nice piece of discarded fish or a chicken bone, and trot back into the jungle to enjoy our treat. The fewer humans we saw, the better. Mother was right: they were unpredictable. Little humans would pull our tails or chase us. Big humans might give us a kick in the belly if we were lying by their porch.

It was best to stay away from these two-legged beasts.

Later, I learned that not all humans dislike dogs. In fact, some *really* like us and keep us in their houses and feed us and take us on long walks. When I was young, I did not realize this. I thought all people despised us.

It took me a while to understand that the people on my island are not bad people. They just grew up in a place that does not accept dogs. Different people have different cultures—some cultures keep dogs as pets and others do not. The people on my island were taught to distrust dogs, just like my mother taught us to avoid humans.

Even though I knew the people on the island could never really like me, I was curious about them and dreamed of one day having a human friend of my own.

Visitors

A year passed and my siblings and I left our mother's side and started living by ourselves. It wasn't so bad. There were long stretches of jungle and beach to explore, animals to see, and lots of food to find (if you knew where to look). There were plenty of three-toed sloths and monkeys in the trees and I would bark loudly whenever I saw them, just to show them *I* was king of the jungle.

I was happy most of the time, but sometimes I felt lonely. The king of the jungle does not always have a lot of friends.

Then one day, my life changed forever. Visitors arrived on my island.

I knew they were from a different place because of the funny way they talked. They didn't sound like any other human I had encountered. They were young humans—but fully grown—and full of energy and laughter.

They arrived by themselves or in groups of two, and they all lived together in a long building with lots of rooms. During the day, the Visitors worked. They cleaned, helped in the kitchen, painted designs on the walls. At night, they would relax—sometimes singing or talking loudly or eating cooked fish and pork. I was curious about these humans and watched them from a distance...at first.

One night, a new Visitor arrived on the island—a young woman with skinny legs and a big backpack. She set her things in her bedroom, walked out into the warm night, and sat on the ground. It was dark and quiet where we lived—no streetlights or cars. She looked up at the stars shining over her head for a few minutes, then dug into her pocket and retrieved a packet of crackers. I watched her from a hidden spot in the trees, hungrily eyeing the crackers. They smelled delicious! I wanted a taste, just a taste. Maybe she would leave a cracker or two in the packet when she threw it away. I could only hope!

I took a few steps toward the quiet young woman and saw her head turn toward me. I froze, hoping she wouldn't chase me away with a stick or throw something at me. She sat still and, to my surprise, called out to me in a friendly voice and beckoned me to come closer.

This confused me greatly. Why would a person want me to come over to her? It must be a trap. Mother always warned me that humans are unpredictable.

The young woman stood and called out again in her soft, friendly voice. She reached out her arm, a cracker in her hand.

I sniffed the air. The salty cracker smelled delicious, and I hadn't eaten all day. Cautiously, I took a step forward, then another. The woman held her hand steady, the cracker held between her fingertips. I strained my neck toward the cracker, grabbed it with my mouth, and scampered away before she could kick or slap me.

The young woman did not move. She just watched me go and let me eat my cracker in peace. A small part of my heart began to soften toward humans.

My Name

As the days passed, I began to trust this group of humans more and more, and I began to understand their strange language. They would call me over and toss me bits of food, or leave me water in a dish. Sometimes they would reach out to pat my head, and I would let them for a few seconds before darting away. Like I said, I was trained to believe that humans are unpredictable and dangerous.

The Visitors lived about a two hours' walk from town, right next to a long stretch of beach. Occasionally, they would all go down to the beach and swim and ride on top of the waves on boards. I would quietly watch them from the jungle and wag my tail.

But one of the Visitors was not so nice. He was older than my new friends and he lived in a big house away from the young Visitors. *He is probably their king*, I thought. One day, the Visitor King brought a couple of men from town to the long building where the young Visitors lived. I was sitting in the shade, trying to keep cool. He pointed at the men, and then he pointed at me. The men nodded and started walking toward me. I tried to run away, but the next thing I knew, I was caught in one of the men's arms and tossed into a boat.

"Help!" I cried, but it was no use. The boat took off across the water, headed for the other side of the island.

After a long time, the boat pulled up to a wooden dock on a part of the island I had never seen before. One of the men grabbed me by the back of the neck and tossed me up on the wooden planks. They got out of their boat and began tying it to the dock. I did not wait to see what would happen next. I ran!

I followed my nose through the jungle, sniffing the air for any trace of my new friends. For four days I wandered across the island, trying to find the Visitors. I was starving and my throat was parched with thirst. On the fourth day, I caught a familiar scent. The Visitors!

Even though I felt weak from my lack of food and water, I began to run. I ran and ran until I finally caught sight of the long building that housed all the young Visitors. When they saw me approach, they began to shout, "Dobby! You're back! Hooray! You're back! Come here, boy! Have a treat. Good, Dobby. Welcome back."

"Dobby?" I thought. "What's a Dobby?" I cocked my head and walked toward my humans. I didn't care what a "Dobby" was, I just wanted some food.

Eventually, I realized Dobby was their name for me. A name! I had always wanted a name. Once I found out I had a name, I couldn't stop saying it to myself. "Dobby, Dobby, Dobby," I would repeat. It sounded like "hobby" or "Bobby." It wasn't too short and it wasn't too long. It was a happy-sounding name, a perfect name.

"Dobby!" my friends would say. "You have such big ears and round eyes…just like Dobby the elf!"

I didn't know who Dobby the elf was, but I wagged my tail anyway. It was nice to have a name; it was nice to feel loved.

Kate

I trusted my new friends a little more each day. I let them pet my fur and take the nasty ticks off my ears. I even let them give me a bath sometimes. When the Visitor King realized I was still hanging around, he shook his head and looked the other way. I was safe for now.

My days with the young Visitors were happy. I loved them all, but my favorite human was the girl they called Kate. She was the girl who gave me a cracker out of her hand on her first night on the island. She was quiet and calm—just like me—and she loved to go on hikes. I would follow her whenever she walked into the jungle, and she would talk to me sometimes as she walked.

"It sure is a beautiful day isn't it, Dobby? Let's see if we can spot some capuchín monkeys, okay? I heard they were right around this spot yesterday."

I would wag my tail in agreement and trot alongside her.

Sometimes Kate would go swimming. This always scared me greatly. What if she got hurt out there? What if she drowned? I had to protect her.

Even though I did not like the ocean waves, I would wade into the water and paddle toward my human. When she spotted me, Kate would stop whatever she was doing, swim toward me, and pick me up in her arms.

"Oh, Dobby," she would say. "I'm all right. You just relax on shore."

She would swim back to shore and drop me off, then she would return to the water. I would watch her for a little while, get scared once more, and try to rescue her again. Kate was always patient with me and took good care of me. One time, she even saved my life.

Coco

There were plenty of lady dogs on the island and I wanted to be friends with all of them. *I am the king canine*, I thought. *Of course every lady dog would love to hang out with me.*

That wasn't always the case. Oftentimes, the female dogs on the island would turn up their noses when I was around and ignore me. I did have a few female friends, however, and I guarded them fiercely. "No one will ever hurt you," I growled. "I won't let any bullies come near."

But Coco did not pay attention to my rules.

Coco was one of the dogs that the Visitors had named. He was a short, muscular dog with white, speckled fur, thick shoulders, and a square head, like a box. He thought *he* was king of the island.

"I can talk to any lady dog I want," he told me. "You can't stop me."

Now, that made me mad. I didn't like to start fights, but whenever Coco was around, I felt like jumping on him and tackling him to the ground. He was aggressive and would not leave me alone.

One time, I was hanging out with my friend, Flora, when Coco walked past us. "She doesn't want to talk to losers like *you*," Coco said. "Come on Flora. Let's go for a walk by the beach."

Flora hesitated.

"Don't go, Flora," I said. "We were having a good time talking."

Flora lowered her eyes. "I'd better listen to Coco. He gets angry when other dogs don't listen to him. Sorry, Dobby."

I watched her go with Coco and felt the hair on my back prickle with anger. Who did Coco think he was?

The next day, a big group of tourists came to the island and stayed in the long building where my friends lived. They laughed and played games and fed me bits of food. I liked them and decided to stay by their sides, rather than look for Flora or my other dog friends.

That night, the group of tourists wanted to go to a bonfire on the beach, and Kate agreed to take them there.

The air was dark when the group set out for the beach. Kate had the only light, and she secured it to her head with a strap. "Let's go!" she said. "The bonfire has already started."

They took off down a dark jungle path. I trotted behind them, excited to be around such nice humans. We had only walked a few feet down the path when I heard rustling beside me.

"What are you doing, sissy?" a growly voice said.

"Nothing, Coco," I snapped. "Just going to the beach."

"I'm coming along too," Coco said. "I'm going to steal your humans away from you, just like your friend Flora."

That comment made me mad, and once again I felt the hair prickle on the back of my neck. I ignored my impulse to give Coco a good chomp and continued to tail the humans. The tourists following Kate walked cautiously down the path, whispering as they went. They were not used to darkness like I was, and it made them nervous. "What's that rustling?" they said.

"Don't worry," said Kate, "it's only the island dogs following us."

Coco thought it was funny to make the humans scared. He growled from the darkness and nipped at my ankles, making me yip in pain. When the jungle path ended and opened up onto the beach, Coco saw an opportunity to go after me without trees and vines getting in the way. He ran past the tourists and leaped onto my back, attempting to tackle me to the ground.

The tourists screamed and scattered.

"GO!" Kate yelled. "Go to the bonfire! It's down that way! I'll take care of the dogs."

The group of tourists didn't hesitate. They scampered down the sand toward the blazing bonfire.

In the meantime, I tossed and turned, trying to get Coco off me. I tried to speak, tried to reason with him, but he would not listen. We tussled and fought all the way to the edge of the water. Coco was stronger than me and managed to pin me down under the ocean waves. He held my throat in his powerful jaws, clamping down until it was hard to breathe. From somewhere above the ocean water I heard a voice.

"Get off him!" the voice shouted. "Leave Dobby alone, you scoundrel! Leave him alone!"

It was Kate. Even though she did not want to hurt Coco, she decided she had to do *something* to save my life. She gave Coco a few swift kicks in the ribs, and he let go of me and rushed away. She reached down, scooped me out of the water, and carried me to shore.

"Oh, Dobby," she moaned, "you're hurt and bleeding. Let's get you back and bandage you up."

I didn't protest as Kate lifted me, cradled me in her arms, and carried me back to her room in the long building. There, she washed out my wounds and set up a bed of blankets so I had a comfortable place to sleep.

Kate saved my life that night; I never forgot it.

Gone

After that night, I grew even more attached to my human. I would follow her closely and sleep outside her door at night. One day, she was acting strangely. Kate and her two friends—K.T. and Julie—were taking things out of their dressers and putting them into backpacks. I observed as they rolled up socks and shorts and swimsuits and put them in the bags. Something was happening. Change was in the air.

The next day, I followed Kate and her friends down to the docks. They often used boats to go away from our island. They would shop at the town across the water and come back with groceries or dog food. Usually, they were never gone for more than an hour or two and I would wait for their return.

Today seemed different. I sensed that Kate, K.T., and Julie were going away for a long time.

When the ferry boat pulled up to the dock, the humans piled inside, pulling their backpacks with them. I stood on the dock as they said, "Goodbye, Dobby. We'll see you after our trip!"

I didn't know where they were going. All I knew was that I didn't want my Visitor friends to leave. They had to be stopped!

As the captain launched the boat, I felt anxious and frightened. I plunged into the water after them!

"Go back, Dobby! Go home!" the girls shouted as I paddled after them.

I continued swimming until a man in a boat grabbed me around my torso and lifted me up. He brought me to shore; I shook the water out of my fur, and watched as Kate and her friends motored away.

For the next two weeks, I was despondent and sad. I didn't know how long my favorite human would be gone and I didn't understand why she would leave me. Didn't she care about me? Would she *ever* come back?

One afternoon, I was lying in the shade at the top of a hill, trying to keep cool, when I heard a familiar voice call my name.

"Dobby! Where are you, boy? I'm back!"

My ears pricked up. It was Kate! I ran down the hill to the docks and greeted her with a big jump and a kiss on her chin.

I also learned a valuable lesson: You should trust the ones you love and believe they will never abandon you.

Trust

My trust was put to the test only a couple months later.

I walked into Kate's bedroom one day to find her sitting on a chair, crying. "Oh, Dobby," she said when she saw me, "I have terrible news. The Visitor King is meeting with important people from the United States next week. These people have put a lot of money into the island to create a fancy resort and the Visitor King wants to make a good impression on them. He has ordered his people to round up all the stray dogs and ship them to a tiny, barren island a few miles from here. That means you, Dobby!"

Kate looked at me sadly. "And what's worse," she continued, "I have to return to America in only two weeks. My six months in Panama are up, and it's almost time to go home. What on earth can I do? I can't leave you in danger!"

I listened to Kate as best I could, but I did not fully understand what the trouble was. All I knew was that she was upset. I hesitated, trying to think of how I could comfort her. I took a step closer, then another. I looked up at her tear-streaked face and gently placed my head in her lap. I had never done this before and Kate looked at me, surprised.

"I love you too, Dobby," she said, and scratched me behind the ears. "We'll figure out a way to keep you safe, even if it means taking you back to America with me next month."

Kate marched out the door and went to talk to the Visitor King. I trotted after her, like usual.

What happened after that was a series of events I only fully understood later, after listening to Kate tell the story many times to her family and friends.

Kate confronted the Visitor King and talked with him until they reached some sort of agreement. Then, she arranged for a veterinarian to visit the island from another town. The vet had to take a forty-five minute bus ride and two boat rides just to reach our island!

"If you want to bring him back to America," the vet told Kate, "he'll have to have a series of four shots, spaced two weeks apart for each round."

"Four rounds of shots, spaced two weeks apart?" Kate cried. "But I will be back in the United States by then!"

The veterinarian shrugged. "You'll have to make arrangements for someone on the island to take care of his shots. Rules are rules."

Kate swallowed and said, "I understand."

Shortly after the vet's first visit, Kate bought me a collar. She put it on me and said, "You're a handsome fellow, Dobby! Now, listen closely. It's important you wear this collar and behave yourself while I'm gone. The Visitor King has agreed to let you stay on the island, as long as I take you home with me as soon as possible. I have to go soon, but I'm leaving money with Julie so she can give you all your medical shots and, eventually, put you on an airplane to the U.S. Can you be a good boy in the meantime?"

I licked Kate's face and assured her I would be a good boy. I would wait patiently until she sent for me. Soon after that, Kate left.

I felt lost for a while, downtrodden because my friend was gone. Fortunately, K.T., Julie, and Julie's dad, Kelly, and his partner, Amy, looked after me. Kelly loved to cook and sometimes gave me bits of hamburger and sausage. I enjoyed the treats, but missed Kate.

Sometimes, I wondered if Kate had forgotten about me. I wondered if I would ever see her again. But, I didn't let myself doubt for long. I trusted her. I knew, deep down, we would see each other again someday.

Reunited

Unfortunately, not all plans work out as smoothly as they should. The weather was hot in Panama that summer, and Julie told me it was too dangerous for me to fly in the cargo hold of an airplane. I had to wait from the end of March all the way to October until the airline agreed it was safe for me to fly in a plane.

That October, Kelly and Amy packed up their things and said, "Okay, Dobby, it's time for us to go."

Kelly attached a leash to my collar (I was still learning how to walk with a leash, but was catching on quickly!) and walked me down to the familiar boat docks. I wasn't too fond of riding in boats, but I trusted Kelly.

From the boat, we took a taxi to a little airport. I was put in a crate in the back of the plane and flew all the way to a big, bustling city. I had never seen so many buildings and cars in all my life!

"We're in Costa Rica," Amy told me. "We leave for the U.S. tomorrow."

The loud noises in the city made me nervous, but I knew in my heart everything would be fine. The next day, I let Kelly and Amy guide me back into my crate. I was loaded onto the airplane, and Kelly called out to me, "Hang in there, Dobby! We'll see you in Texas!"

The doors shut and everything went dark. I settled into my crate, listened to the roar of the airplane engines starting, and thought about finally seeing Kate again.

I later learned that while I was on the airplane, Kate and her parents were making the long drive from Minneapolis, Minnesota to Dallas, Texas. Kate was excited to see me, but her parents wondered what was so special about a dog that caused their daughter to go through so much effort to bring him to America. They wondered if I would recognize Kate or if the plane ride would make me agitated and mean.

The weather over Texas was stormy that day. I felt the airplane rock and jolt. "This is the captain speaking," a voice said above me. "We will be diverted to New Orleans for a while to wait for this weather to clear up. Sorry for the delay."

The voice stopped. I felt nervous again, but remained as calm as I could. Kate had asked me long ago to be a good boy, and I was determined to do my best.

After landing in New Orleans, we waited for the storm to pass. And waited. And waited some more. I grew drowsy and thirsty. Finally, we took off for Dallas.

Kate and her parents were waiting in the airport, pacing around, hoping I was okay. I wish I could have told them, "Yes! I'm fine. I trust the people around me to bring me to safety."

When the airplane finally landed and I was wheeled out of the cargo hold, I caught a familiar whiff in the air. Kate? My human? I trembled with excitement.

"She's here, Dobby," Amy whispered into my crate. "You'll see her soon."

I waited calmly as Kelly wheeled the crate through the airport. I passed through a doorway and heard a voice that made my heart go thump-thump in time with my tail.

"Dobby? Is that you? Dobby!"

I instantly recognized the voice and began pawing at the door. Kate! She was here! My best human friend in the whole world was with me again!

When Kelly opened the door of my crate, I jumped out and ran to Kate, leaping up and down, wagging my tail furiously, smiling a big toothy grin. Kate bent down and hugged me, crying happy tears that I licked off her cheeks.

The journey had been long and tedious, but it was all worth it.

Kate and her parents drove me back to Minnesota the next day. I sat in Kate's lap almost the entire time, nuzzling against her skin, breathing in her familiar scent. I never wanted to be separated from my human again.

That was seven years ago, and I have been happily living in Minneapolis ever since. Kate and I go for plenty of walks; I love chasing squirrels and rabbits, running around in the local parks, and hanging out on restaurant patios. Sometimes, a person will approach Kate and say, "What a handsome dog you have! What breed is he?"

Kate will shrug and say, "I'm not sure. He's from Panama."

"Panama?" the people always gasp in disbelief. "How on earth did you find him in Panama?"

Kate will smile quietly, stroke my head, and say, "I didn't. He found me."

The End

Today...

Dobby has been living in the United States since 2010. He has adjusted nicely and has made many friends, both human and canine.

Dobby loves hiking, especially in the forests of Minnesota.

At home, he can often be found lounging in the backyard, watching squirrels, eating the occasional piece of cheese, or snuggling with Kate...

...and Kate could not ask for a better friend.

Acknowledgements

Dobby's story was made possible by the hearts and hands of many people.

Thank you for the support of my Panama people—all the fellow interns and guests who loved, fed, and cared for Dobby. I am especially grateful to Julie and Katie T. for arranging all of Dobby's veterinary care after I had to leave the island. Thank you to Amy and Kelly, who were absolute rock stars and hauled my special little pup through four airports and three countries. Dobby's story exists because of you all.

Thank you to my endlessly supportive parents, who volunteered to join me on my road trip to Dallas to pick up my friend.

Thank you to those who have looked after Dobby when Eric and I were away, especially Annette and Josh, who have housed him on multiple occasions.

Thank you to Eric, who adopted Dobby without hesitation and takes him on long, meandering walks in our neighborhood. Dobby doesn't warm up to many people, but he's smitten with you.

Thank you to the women in She Writes, for their keen eyes and well-placed comments.

Finally, thank you to Dobby, the best companion a person could ask for. You're patient, sharp-as-a-whip, an excellent snuggler, and always up for an adventure.

About the Author

Kate Bitters is the pen name of Kate Leibfried. She is the founder and president of Click Clack Writing, LLC, which helps individuals and businesses express themselves through words.

Kate has written two novels and two children's books.

As a ghostwriter, editor, and book coach, Kate has worked on forty-five (and counting) different manuscripts.

When she's not writing, Kate can be found biking, hiking, and camping with her wonderful companions, Eric and Dobby.

www.KateBitters.com
www.ClickClackWriting.com

A NOTE ON THE ARTWORK

All artwork in this story was created through Painnt, a program designed by Moonlight Apps, LLC. The illustrations were created from the author's actual photographs.

Copyright© 2017 Kate Leibfried

www.ingramcontent.com/pod-product-compliance
Lightning Source LLC
Chambersburg PA
CBHW042218050426
42453CB00001BA/7